EXAMPLES OF HANDWRITING

1550 - 1650

EXAMPLES
OF
HANDWRITING
1550-1650

compiled by

W. S. B. BUCK

Published by

SOCIETY OF GENEALOGISTS

14 Charterhouse Buildings

London EC1M 7BA

First published 1965

Reprinted 1973, 1982, 1985

(c) Society of Genealogists 1965

ISBN 0 901878 54 5

Printed in Great Britain by
Parchment Oxford Limited

INTRODUCTION

The following notes fall into two main sections, namely an Alphabet of single letters; and secondly an extension thereof into an Alphabetical arrangement of the commoner Christian Names of the period A.D. 1550-1650.

To the above is attached a table of Confusibilia, a short list of Abbreviations, and words commonly found in Parish Registers, and a collection of Surnames, illustrating various points.

Virtually the sole source has been the Parish Register of Froome Selwood in Somerset, from which examples have been taken. The earlier portions of this Register were evidently copied in one hand at about 1598, when a number of different hands appear.

The object has been to include as many varieties as was practicable, so as to form a nucleus for reference, and this applies both to the formation of single letters, and to the spelling of Christian Names.

Finally a short selection of Place Names, all taken from a Calendar of Hampshire Wills, has been included as an exercise for those who like puzzles.

Some Hampshire Place Names

Alderton; Aldershott; Andover.

Brokenhurst;

Droxton; Christchurch.

Emsworth; Eastleigh;

Elwat; Highclere, Ettyholt; Salibourn

Lostthead: | network.

Buston; Dinston

Purbright | Burrley

Greatleare; Suthamptun, Houghton

Near Thames: Broughley

3

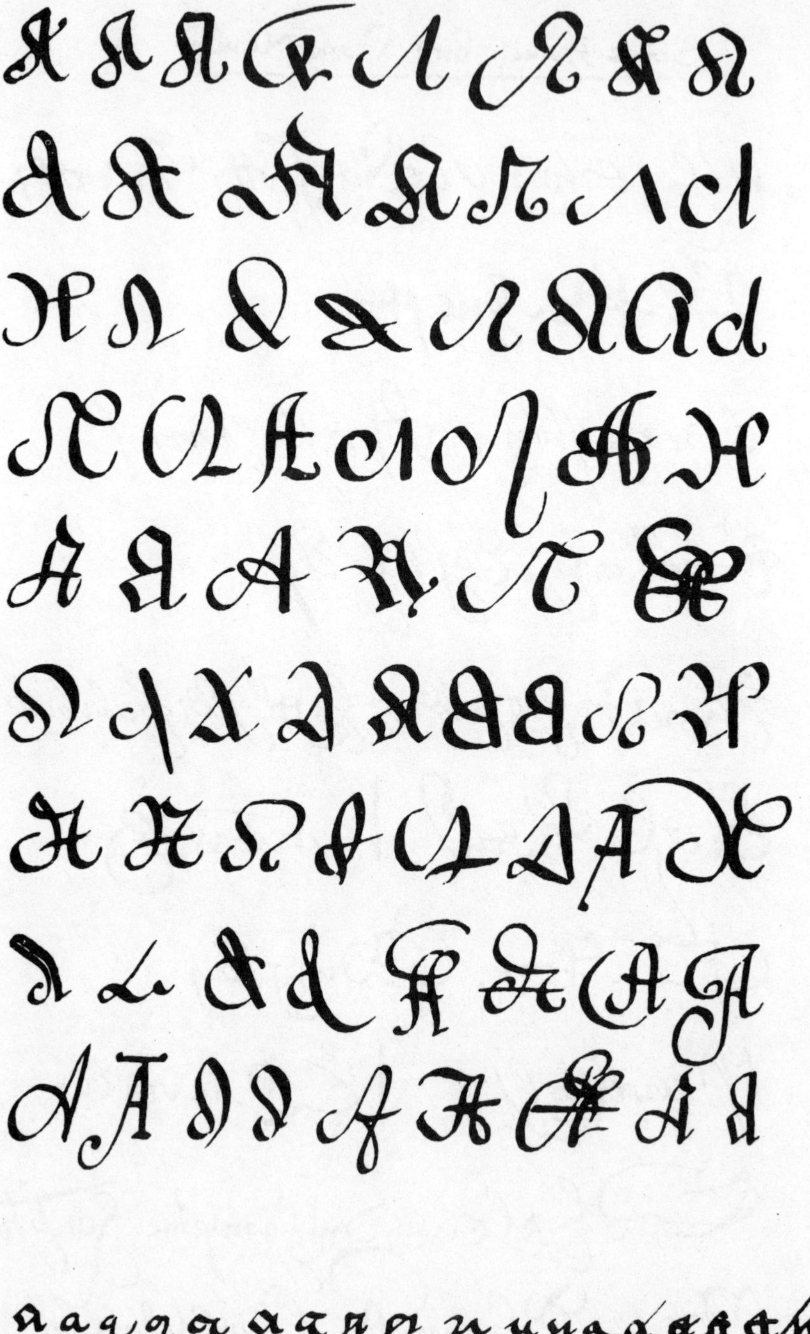

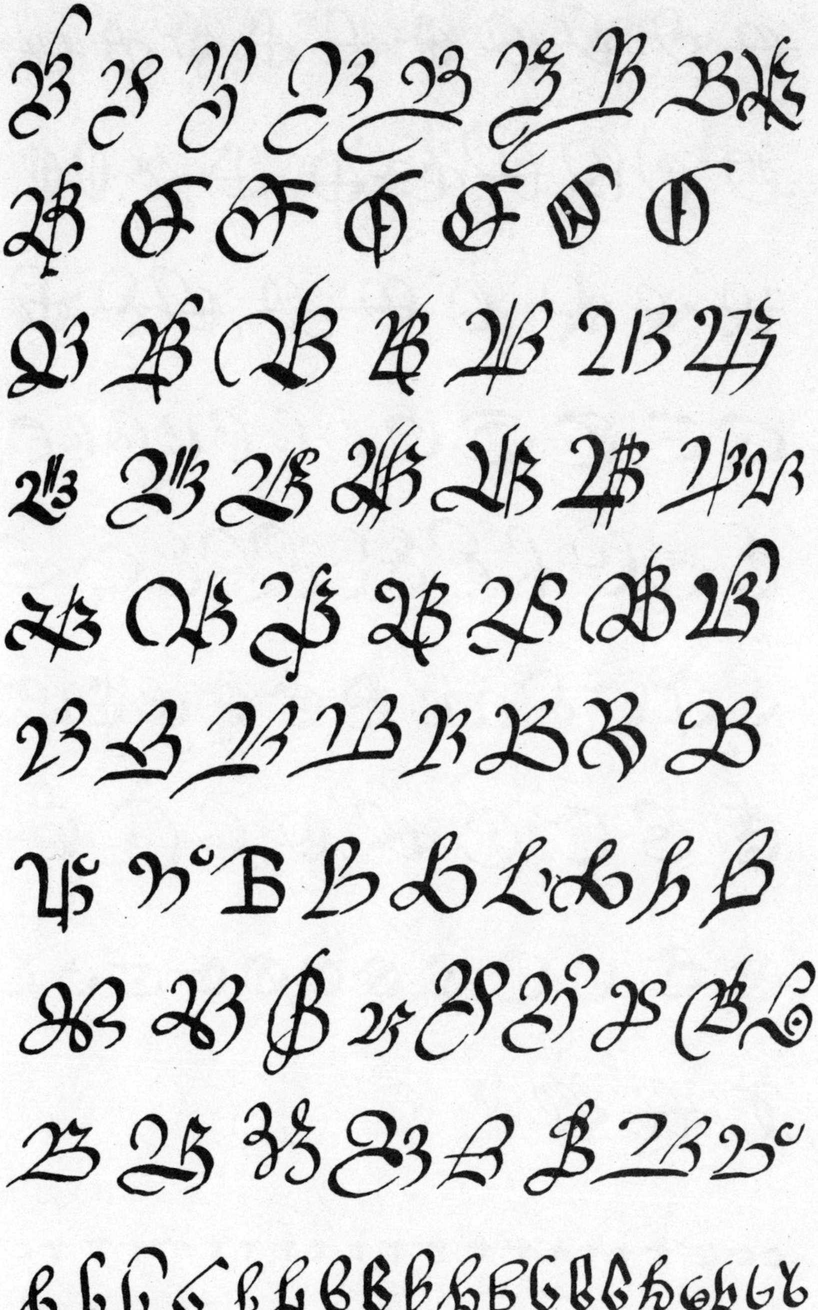

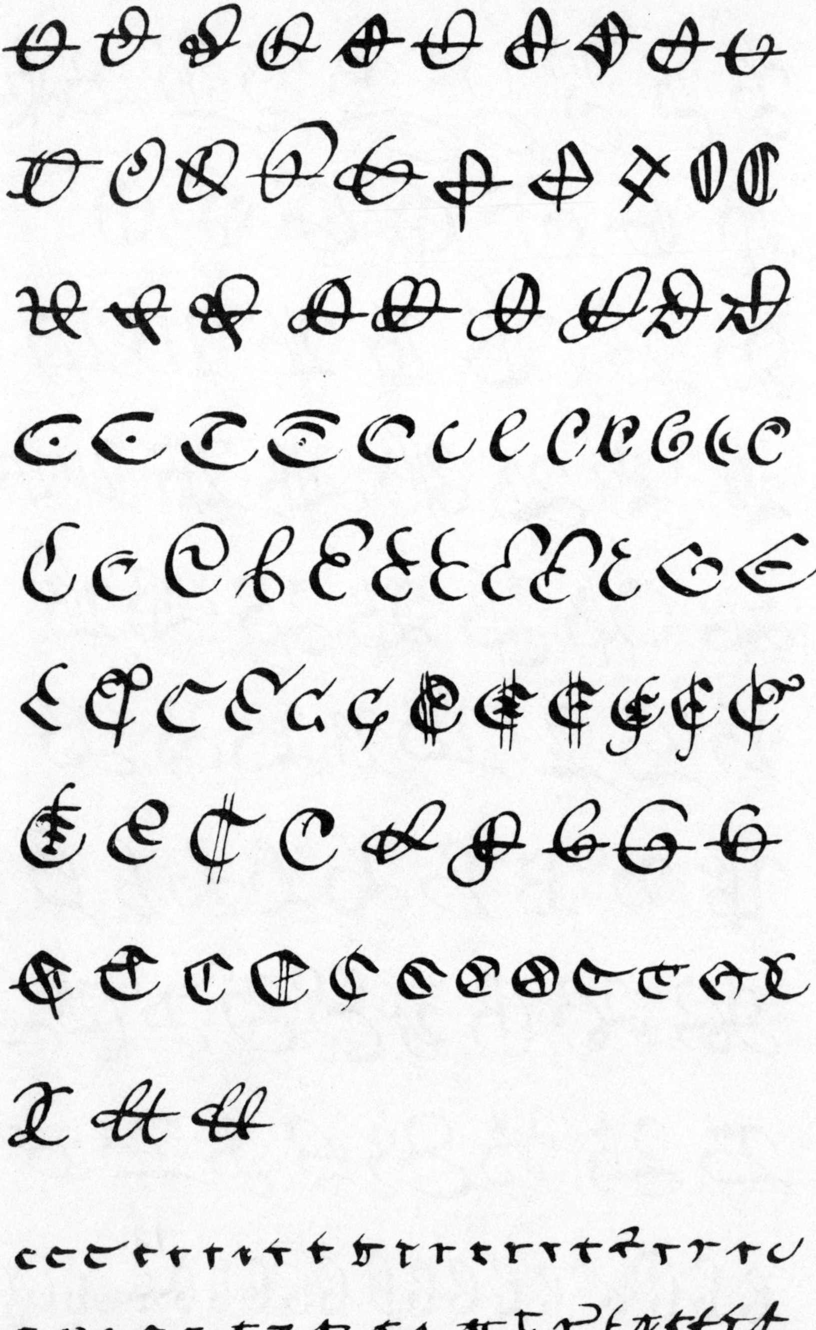

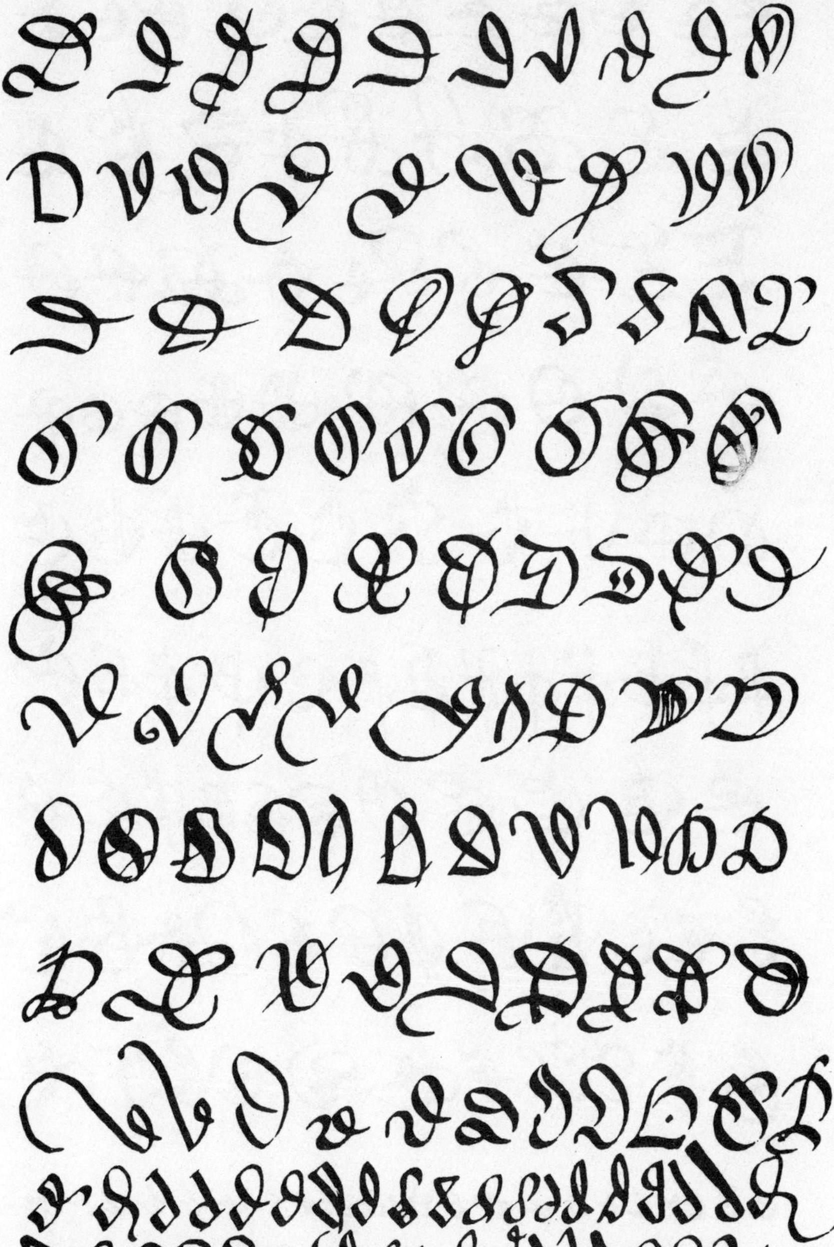

8

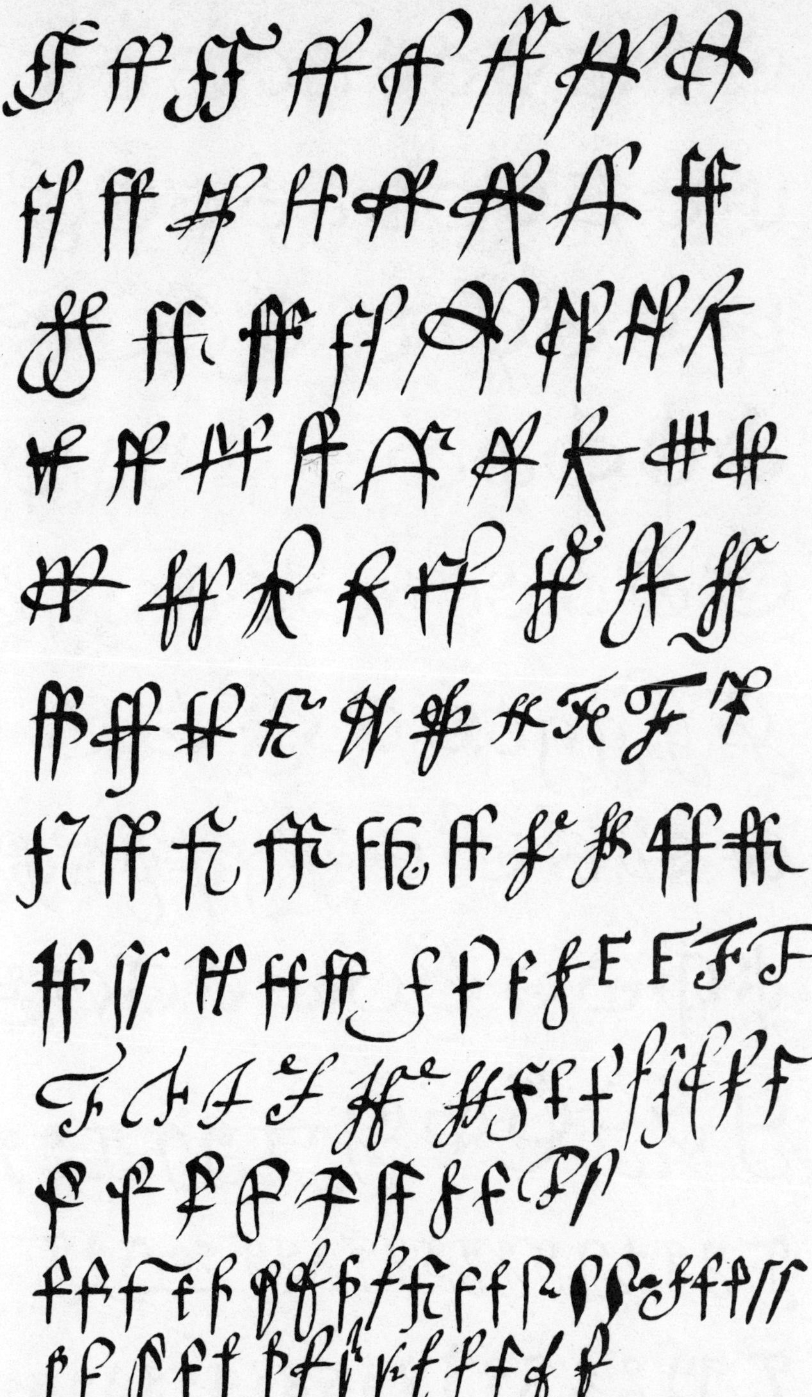

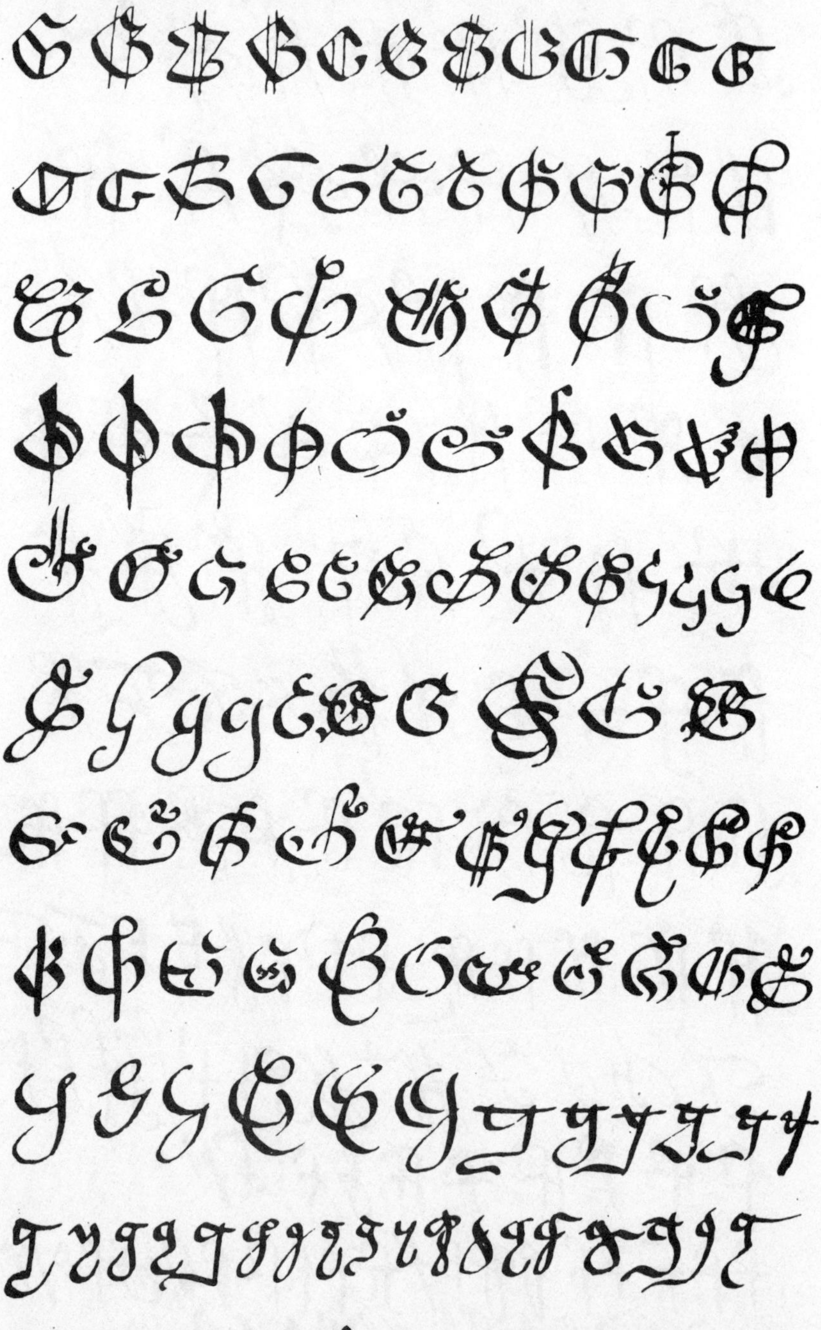

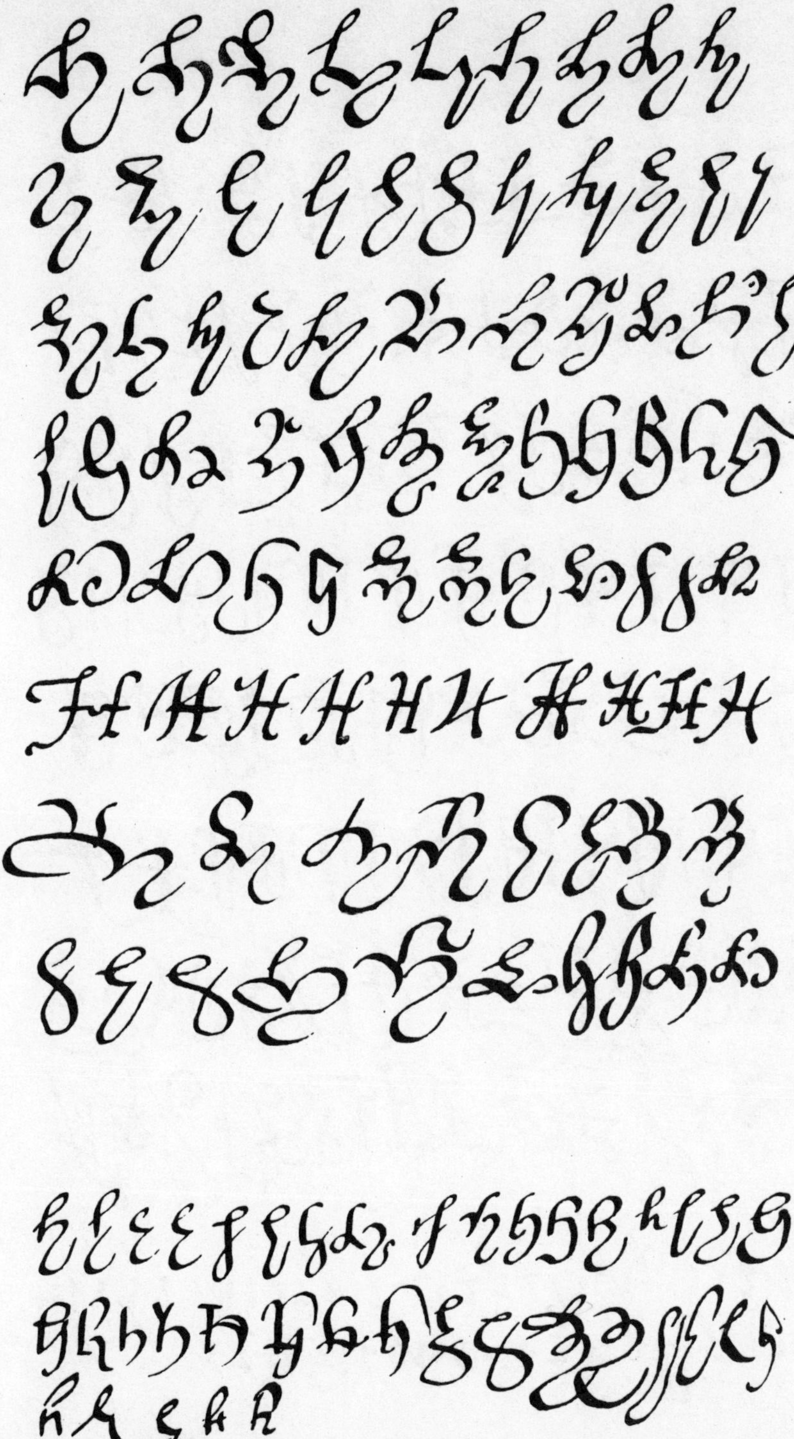

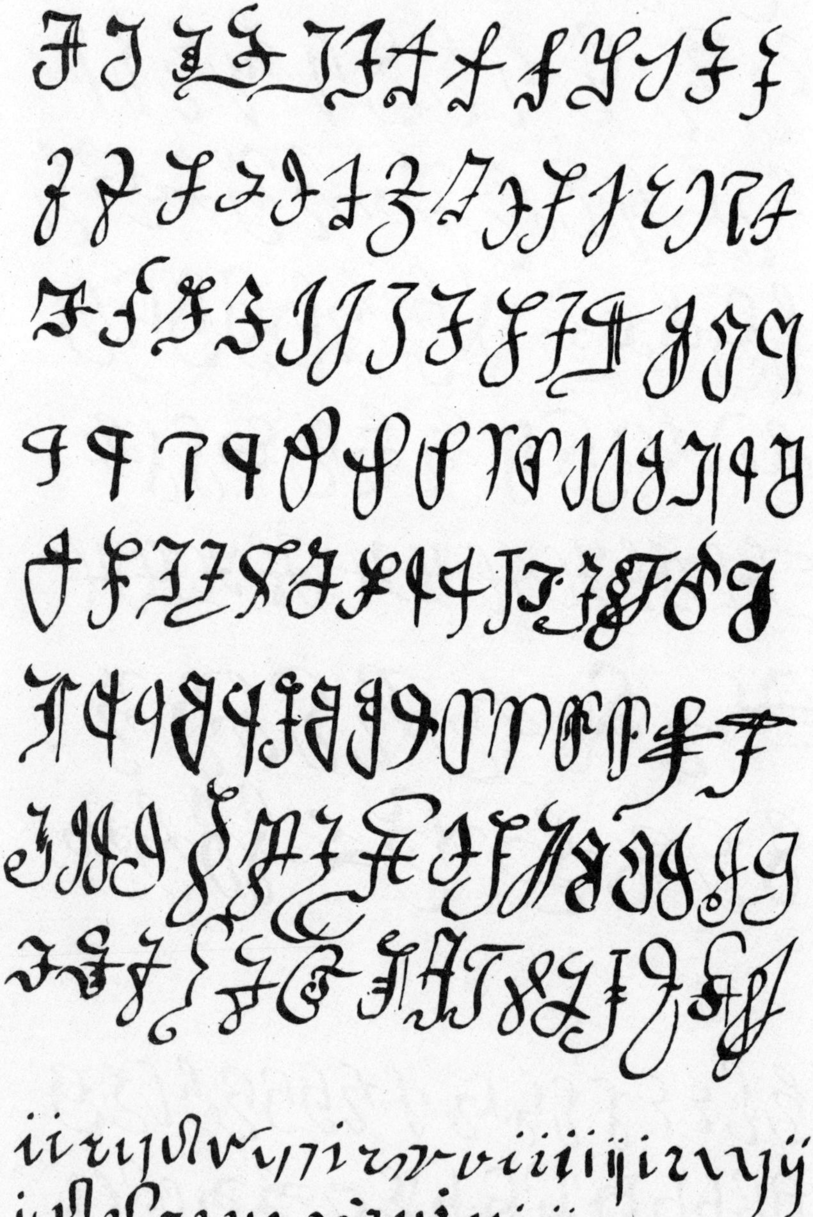

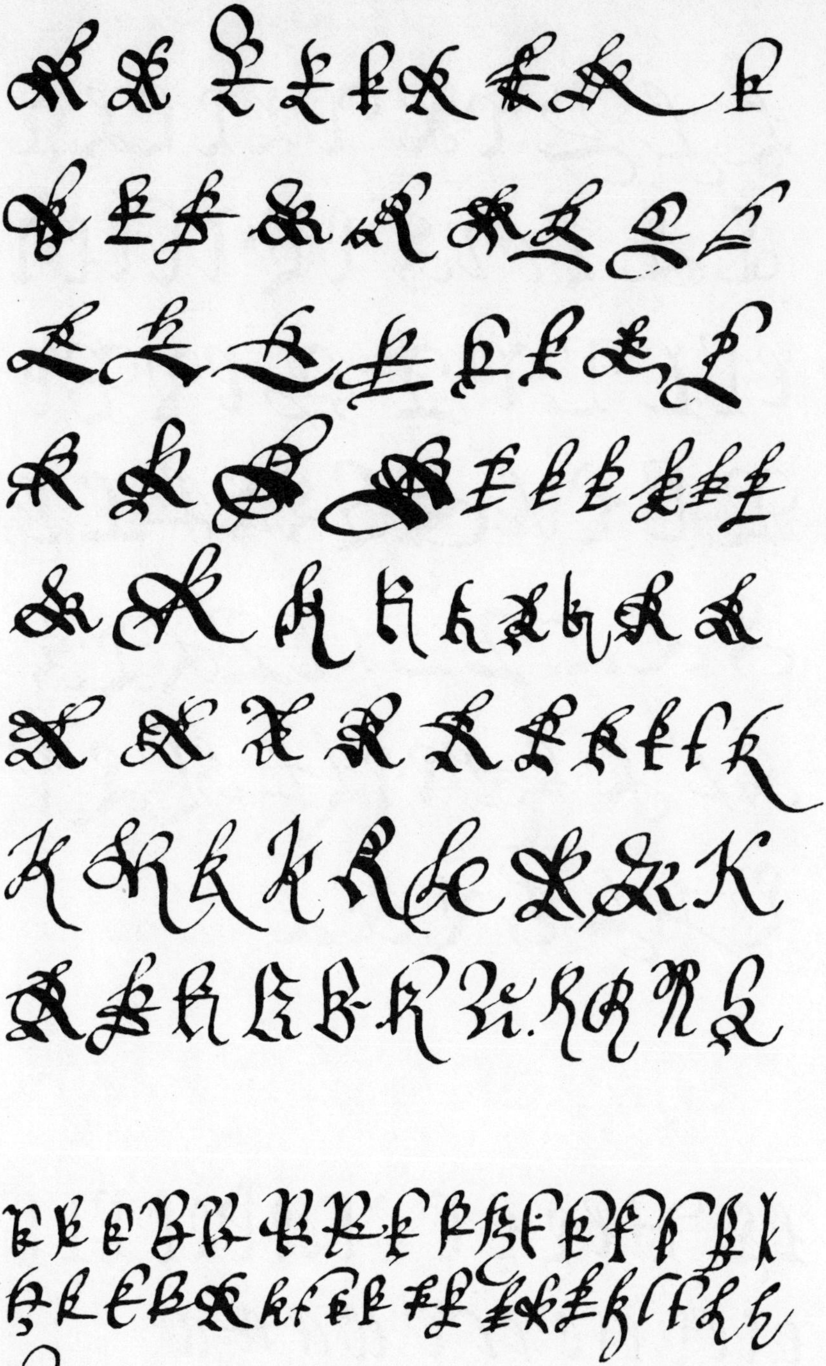

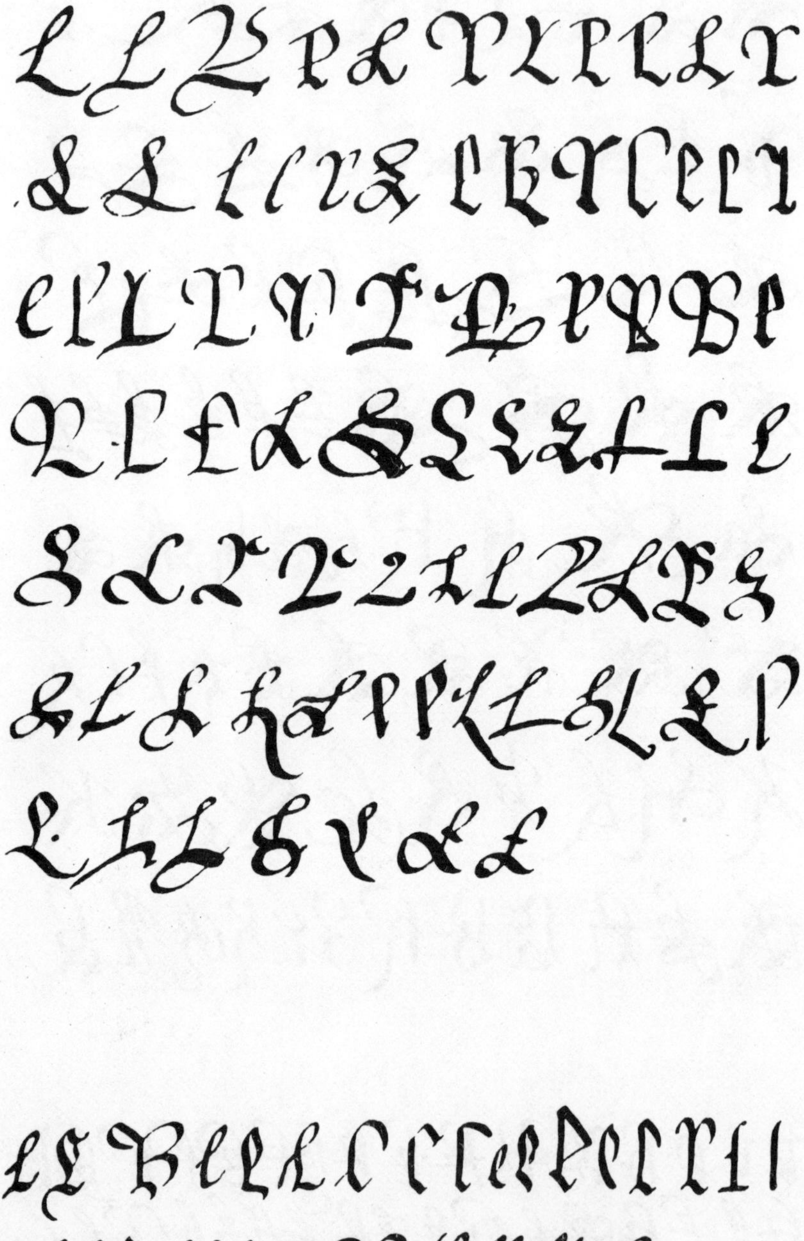

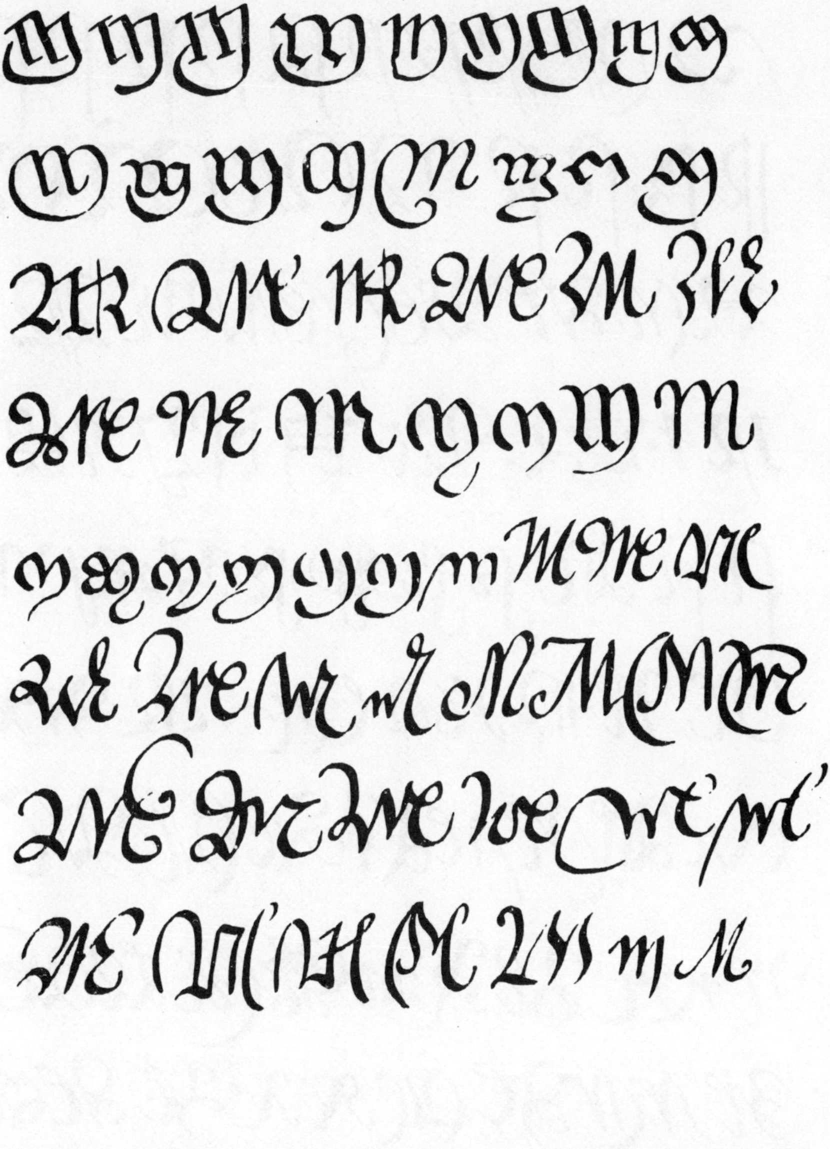

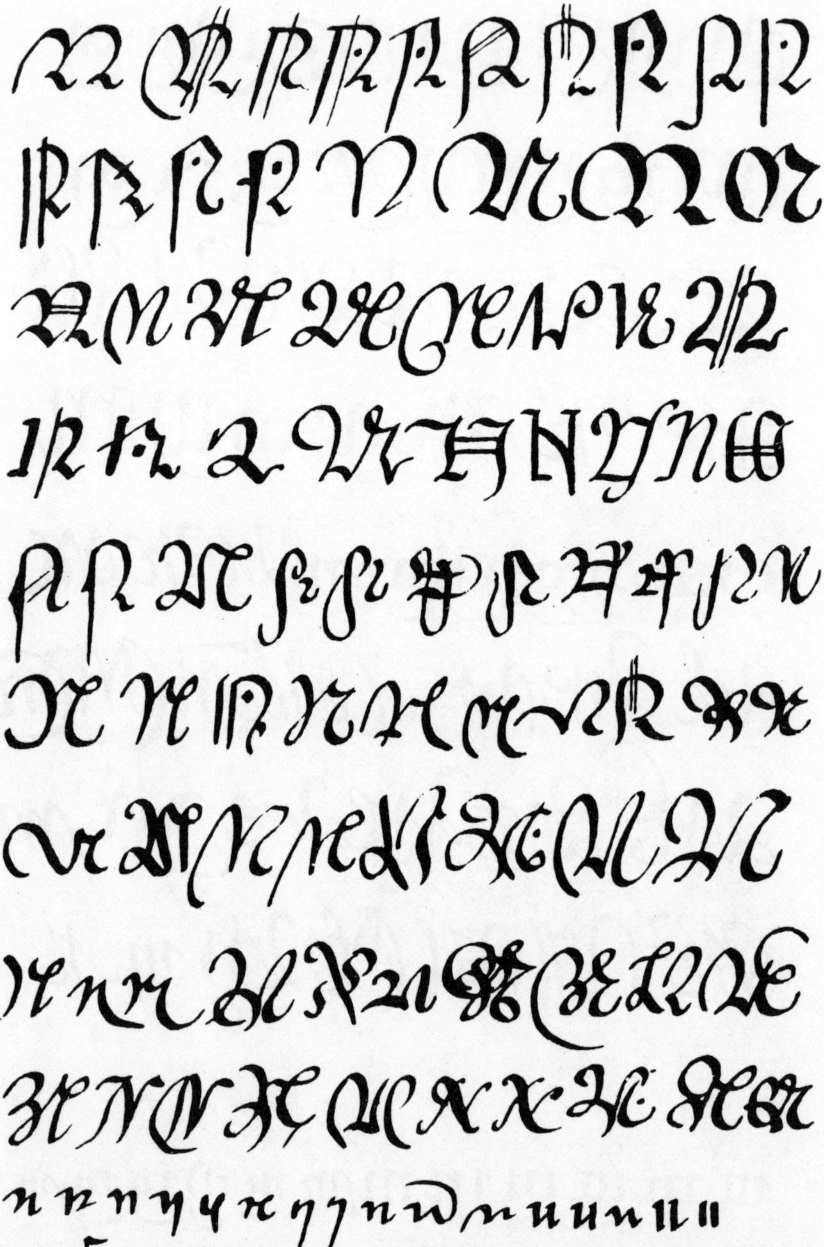

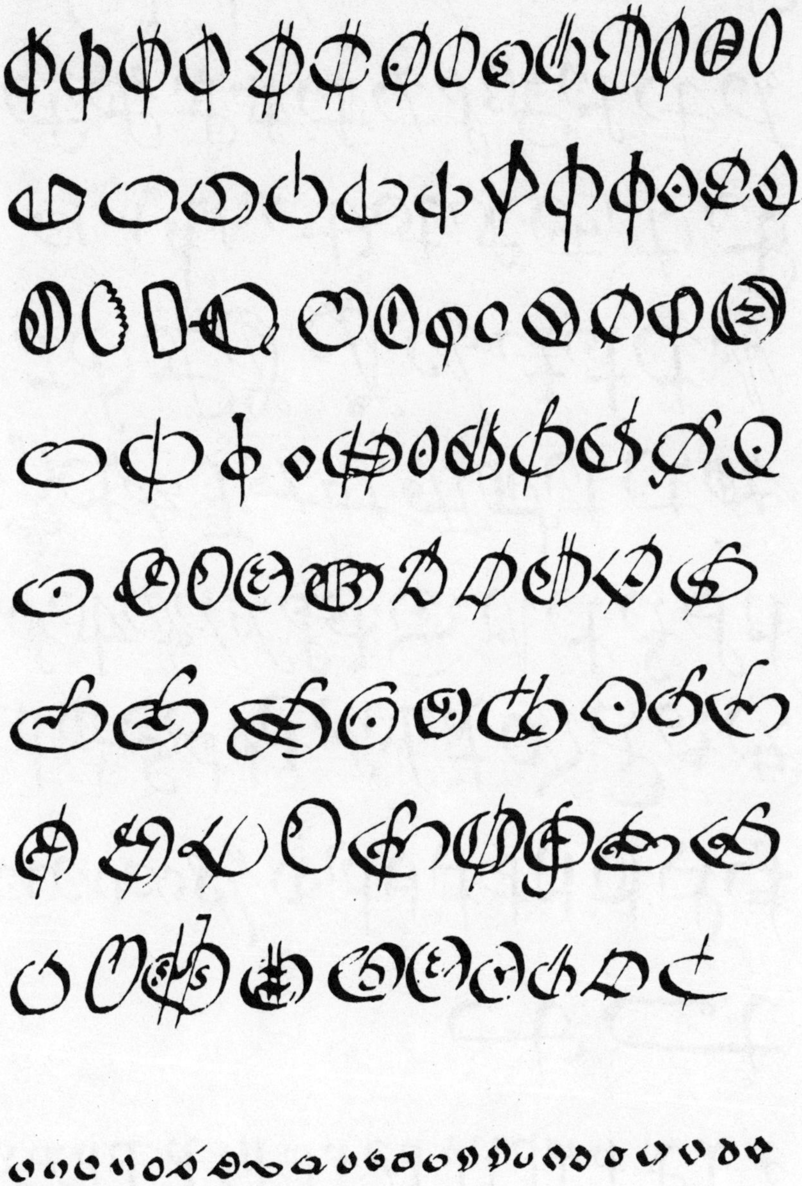

Pro

Per

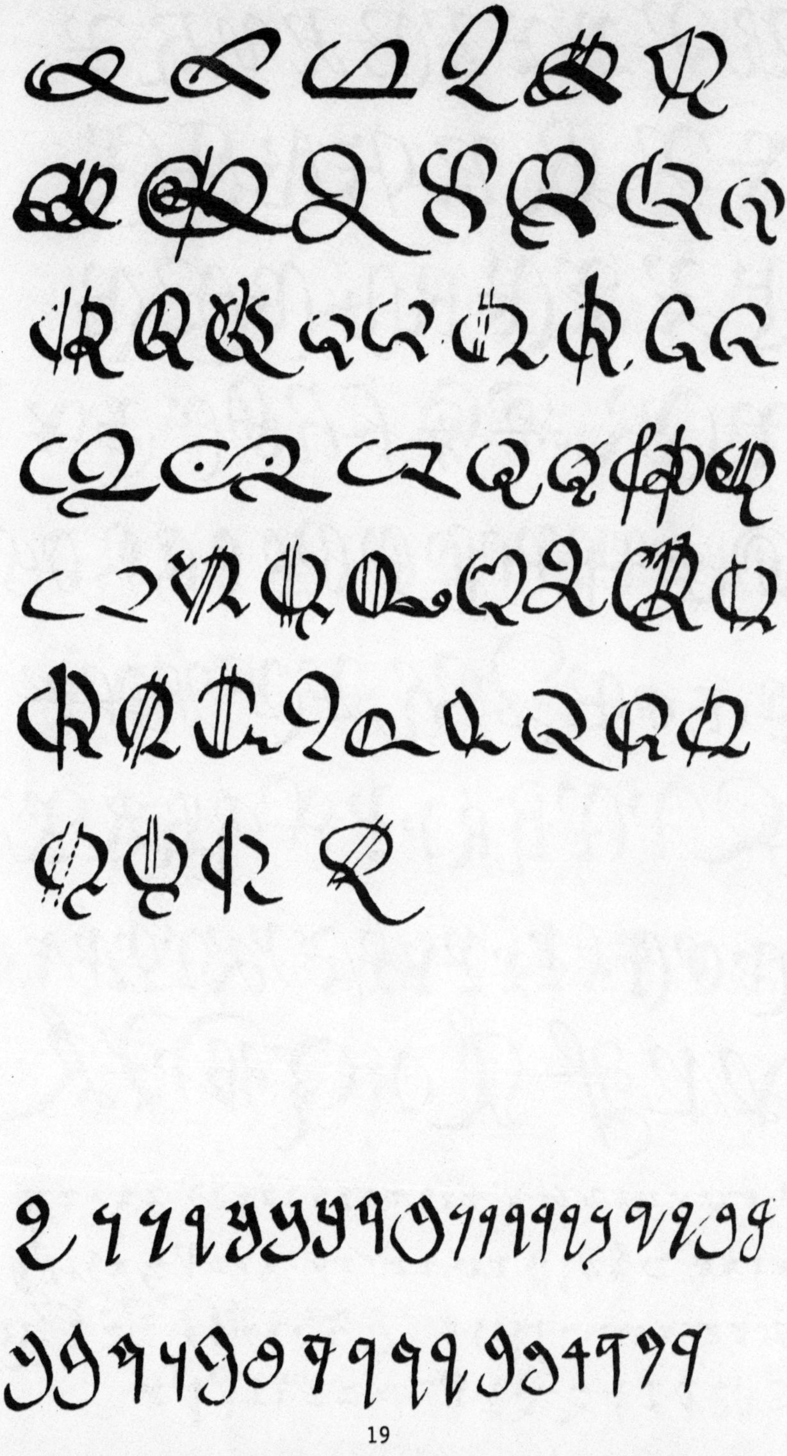

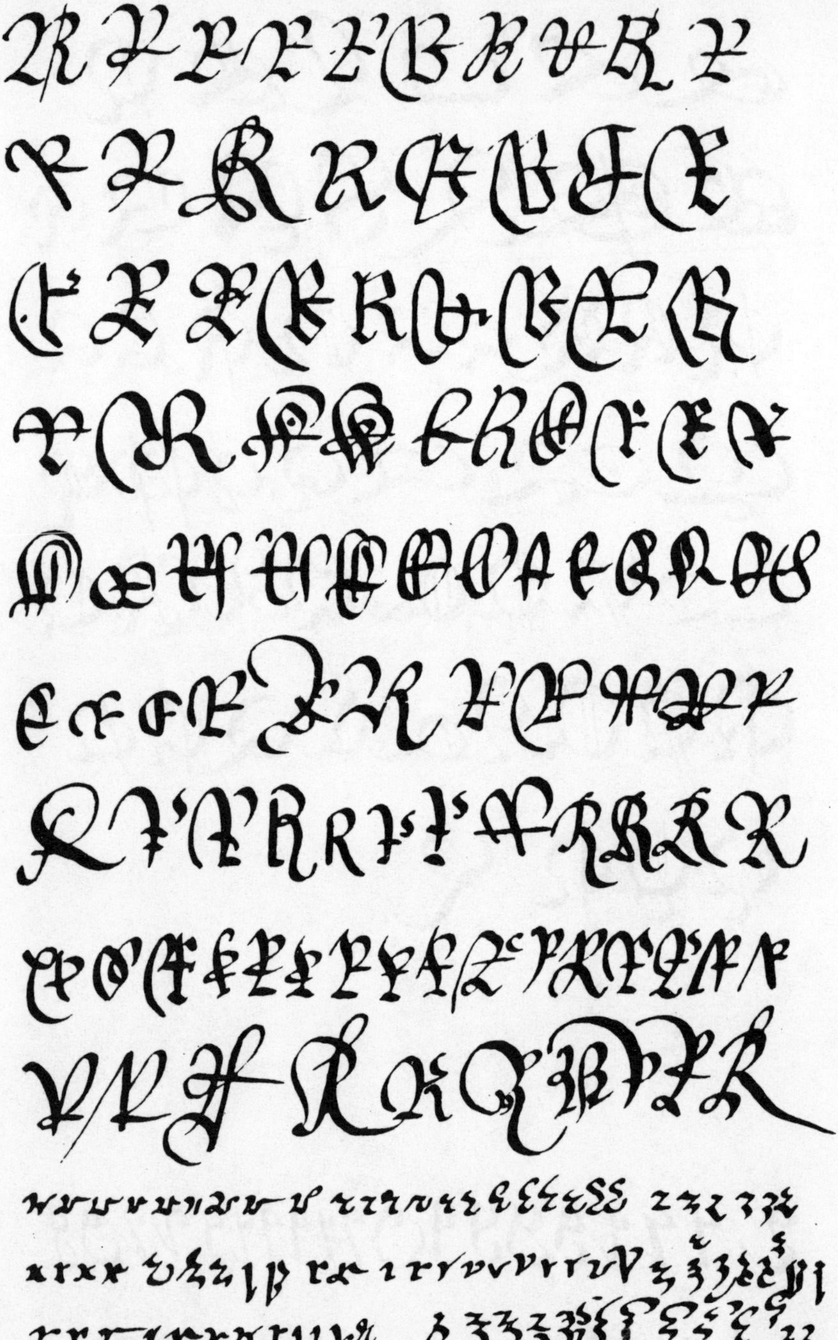

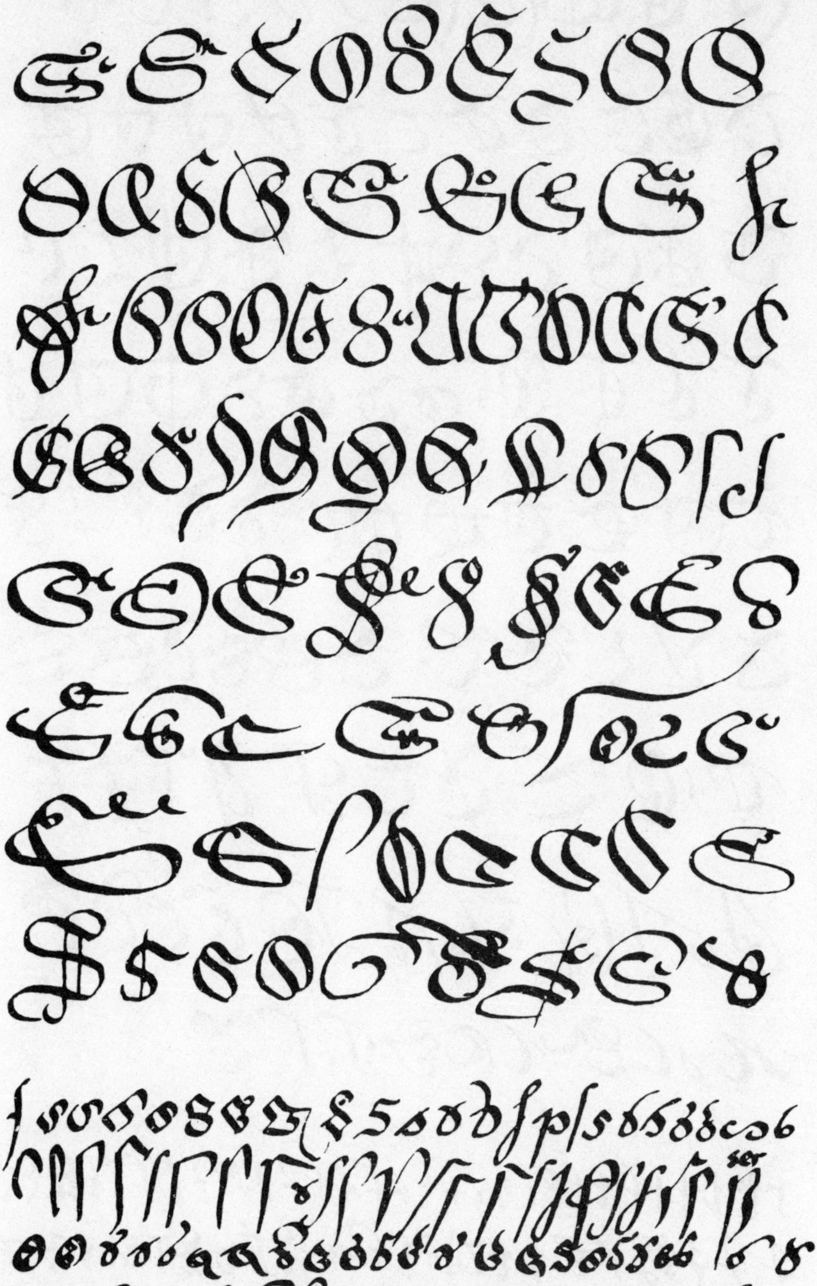

22

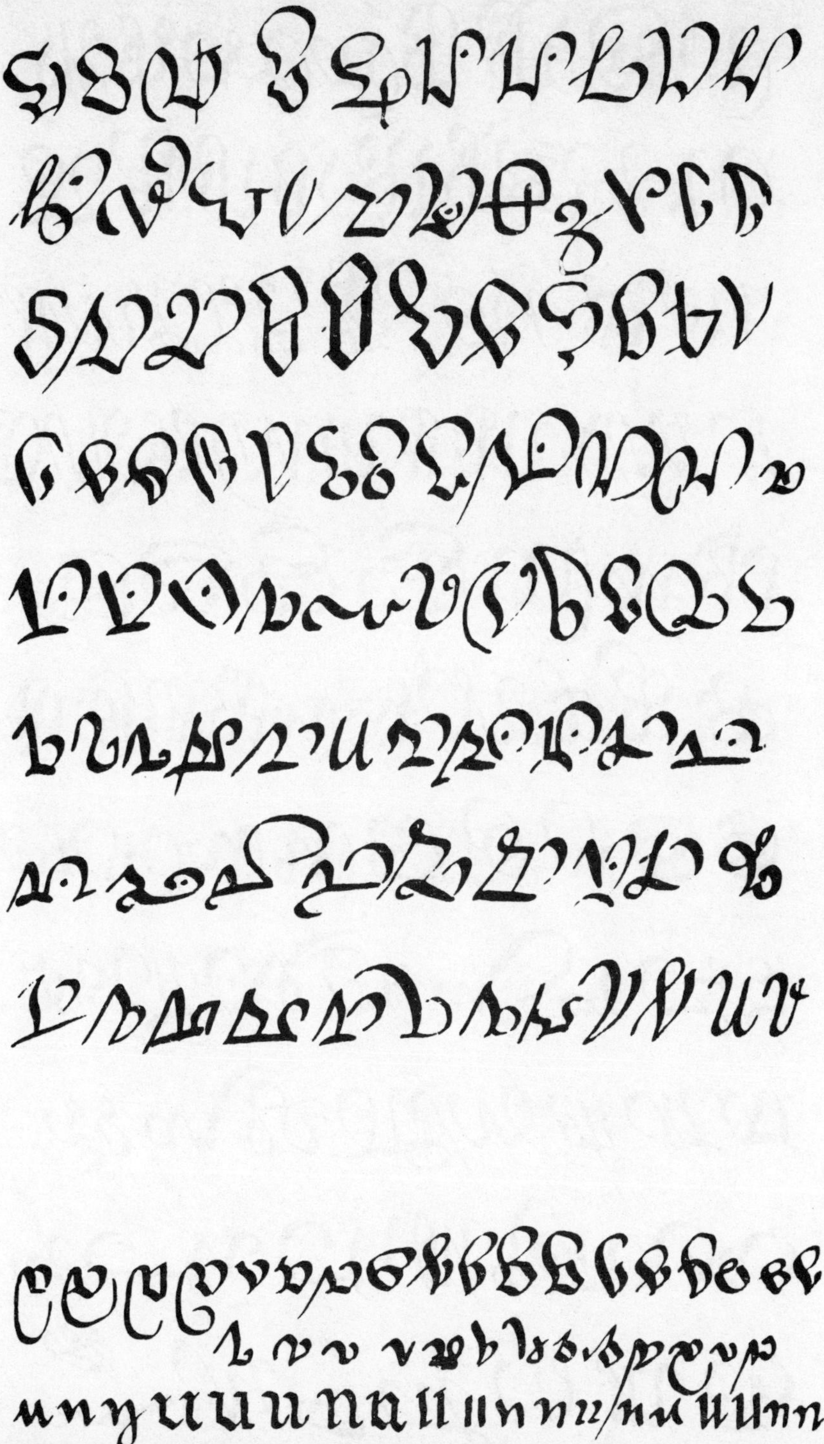

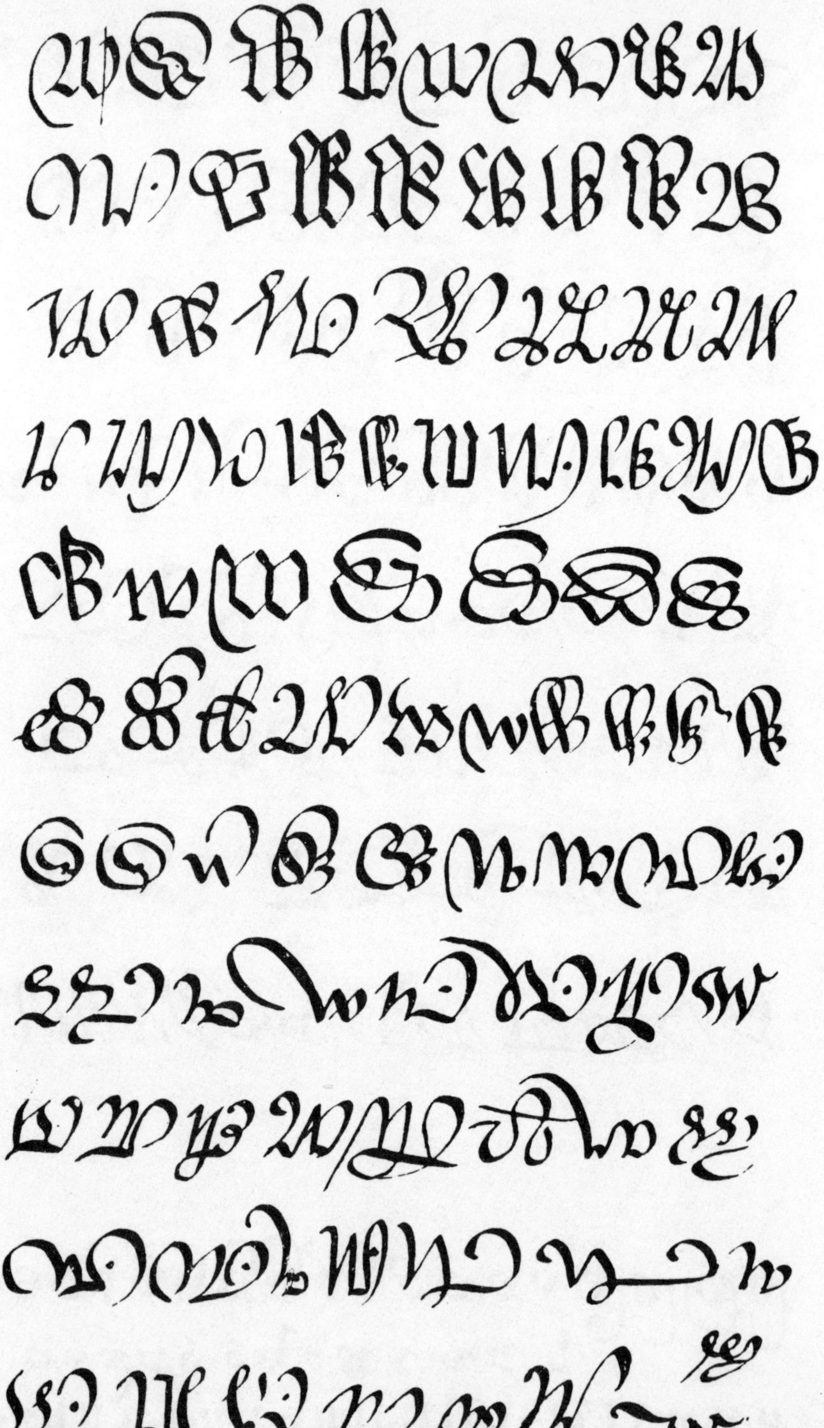

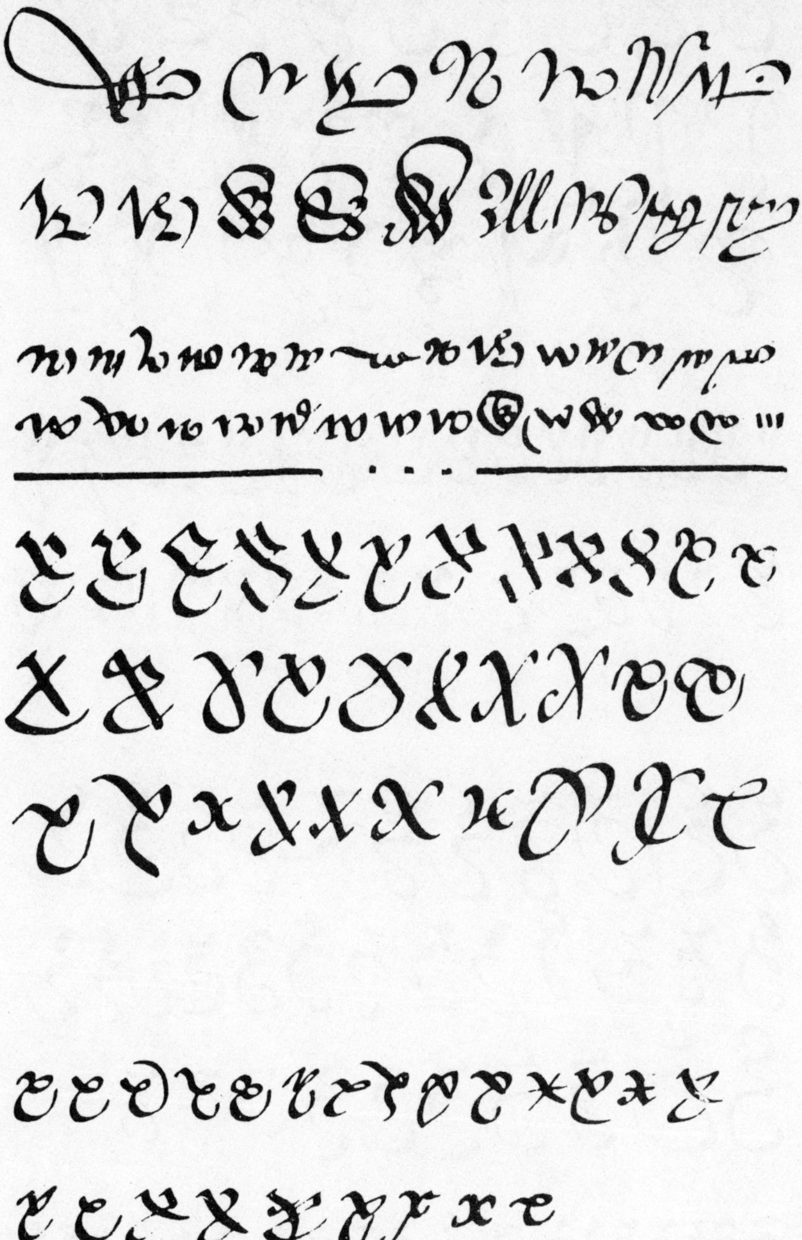

26

Abadnegoo

Abole Abole Aboll

Abigalia Abygall Abigalle

Abigall Abigaile

Abrah Jamus Jbrahom Abram

Adam Adamus Adam Adams

Adrianus Adrianus Adriana

Agatha Agneta Agattis Annis

Agnis Agnes Agnes Agnis

Alang Allams Allen

Alexander Alix Calexsandu

Alexander Alexander

Aquila   Aquila   Aquila

Atheus   Arthur   Arthurus   Arthur

Arthur   Arthur   Arthur

Astrea

Aubrey

Audry   Audrye   Audry

Austine   Juston   Huston

Augustine   Augustino

Avis   Avis   Avisia   Avisa

Avis   Avitia   Aviria

Avelin   Aveling   Evelina

Alce Alles Allese Alicia Alic

Alicia Alice Alyce Alyce Alice Alice

Alys Alisia Allice Alis Alicia Alice Ales

Ambros Ambrose Ambrose Ambrose Ambrus

Amia Amia Amia Anne Amos

Anchora Anatorcta Antoret

Andreas Andreas Androwse

Andrew Andrew Andrews Andrew

Angell Angella

Ann Anne Anne Anna Anne Anne

Anthoni Anthonye Anthonius Anthonye

Anto Anthonye Antonye Anthonye

Anstie Anstis

Balthasar Balthasar

Barborowe Barberye Barbra

Barbourye Barbara

Barnabas Barnabas

Bartholomeus Barthol Bartholmew

Bartol

Basilia Bazill Bazoll Bazoll

Bettowes Bettinea Bettowis

Benedict Benedict Benedick Benedick

Bendick & Benetta Benidork

Beniamin Benyamen Beniaminus

Beniamino Benian Beniamin

Barnard Berndus barnard

Blanch Blanch, Blanch Blanch

Brian Bryan Brianus Bryan

Bridgott Brigott Brigitta Brigeata

Brigiet Bridgat Bradgott Brigida

Bridgott Bridgat Brigett Briguta

Carolus   Caro

Carolus Carolus

Cassandra Cassandra

Catharina Matherina Catherine

Chatorina Catherine Cutherine

Catherson Hutherine

Cril

Cecilia Cecely Cicilia Cissolly

Cicilia Cissell Cicilia Cicilley

Cysley Cysley Cisley Cissolly

Cicilia Cisley Cydley Cicilley

Cissilla Cecely Cisley Cyslie

Cicilia Cistoly

Charytys Charitie Charitie Charity

Charitas Charitys Charitie

Carolus Carolus

Harold os Charles Carles Charly

Charles Charals Charles Carls

Cristaboll

Christiana Christian Cristian Cristia

Christian Cristina Christian Christien

Christian

Christopher Christophorus Christo͂

Cheistover Cristopher Cristofer Crystopher

Clara

33

Clarica Elarica

Clemont Clement Clemant Clement

Constaurd Constaurd Constantia Constant

Cordelia

Cornelis Cornelius Cornelious

Cuthbartus Cutbeard Cutbartt

Cudbartt Cudbert Cutbeard

Daniell Daniel Daniel Daniell Daniel

David David David David

Danide Davide David Davi

Dvans DEans Idanis

Debora deborah

Denis Dionis Dionis Dinis

Dinysia

Degory

Diana   Dinah   Dynah

Deonisia Dionysia Dionisia

Dominik

Dorras

Dorathia Dorothea Derothr

Dorothia Drothea Doratey

Doratho Doritey Dorraphia

Doriphia dorothea Doritey

Doritto Doryte y Dortho

Dorsabella

Innston Donston

Cadok Edtha yedek Edytho

Editha Edihu Editz Eddath

Edath Eddoth Edith Iditha

Edmond Edus Edmondus Edmont

Edward Ead. Edri Ed Ehad

Eadward Ead Edus Edus Edus

Edward Edurd Edus Edus

Edwyn Edwyn Edwind

Egidius Egidius Egidius

Ogidius Egidius Edidius

Elap Elin

Ebinezer

Elenor Eulnur Elinora Elinor Elmr

Elinor Elnr Elinora Elona

Elnur Eallenor Elena Elonur

Elnor Elinor Elnor Elenor Elionor

Ellir Eliz Eliab Eliab Elias

Elizeus Elizeus

Elizabeth Eliz Elizabetha Elifaboth

Elizabeth Elfaboth Elizaboth

Ema Eme Emotto

Enoch Enoch | hyuffos

Eva Eva

Edannd Evan Evand

38

ffaith ffaith ffayth fayth Faith

ffardinand

fides   ff obe (see P.)

fflorence   fflorentia

ffortune Fortunatus ffortungt ffortund

ffrauncis ffrauncesca ffrauncisto

ffrancis Arauntisch Arauncesd

ffrauncisch ffrauncesca

ffranke

ffer Arnolde ffrisrick Friswith ffriswith

ffrisoll   ffroge

Gabriell Gabrill gabrill Gabrill

Gabrill

Galfrid Galfridus

Johry Johny

George Georgius Georgius

George gorg gorg George

Georgij Groge Georg gorgo Geo

Gerard

Gartrid gartrin gartrm Gartrud

Gartroths Gartory Gartry gartry

Garteret Gharstory Gertrud Gartand

Gosford

Gilbertus Gilbtus Gilbert gilbrt

Gilbart Gilbard Gochard

Gily Gylos Giolle Goille Giells

ydukov

gerar Greard Gwaria grar

Grarian) grate Graria

Grigory Grigory Grigory

Griffin

Gundo Guy

Hana Hamar Hana Hanna
Hana Hanah Hañuh Hanna

Honory Henrivus Hendry Hour
Honory Henry Henrit Edmy
Henring

Hester Heldow hoster Hoffer
Hoffer Doctor Heffter
Hester Hoster Heyrthen
Hynor Honor Honor
huge Hugh Hugh hugh Howe
Hugo Hugh hugh Hugh Houg

Eumfridus Lymprio hymphin

hymphio Humfrich hymfruds

Vnfio Vnfu Vmphuid

Innocent   Ingrlin

Izabella Isabella Izabella Isabella

* Isaar Izak Isaac Isaack Isaar

Isaar Isacc Isaar Isak Isako Isaack

Izak Izak Isak Isaac Isacke

Isaiah Isayas Isaiah Esaiah

Israell Israel   Izt

* Isaarhus

Jacob Jacob? Jacobus Jacob Jacobus
Jacob?

Jamy

Jan Jann Jaan Jannd Jand Jant
Jana Jana Jaine

Jesper Jasper Josper Jasper
Josery Josseriu   Joghtee
Jeremiah Jeremiah Hieronymiah
Jerimy Jeromy Heronimy Jeromd
Heronimus Jerom Jurmd Jeromy

Jesse

Jenken Jynkyn Jinkin Jynken
Jentenq

Jono Jone Jone Jont Jons John

Johanna John Joanna Johan

Joss Job ⌐ Jonathan

Johannes John Joh Joh

Johi Johs John Joh Johnfris

Jonas   Joell

Josephus Joseph Joseph Hus Joseph

Josias Jossias Johsias Fosseus

Josias Josias Jsias Josyas

Joice Joyce Joyce Joices Joyss

Joyes Joyes Joyce Joyes

Judeth Judeth Judeth Judith Judeth

Julian Jullian Juliana Julliany

Katherin Katherin Katherine

Katherin Katherina Katherin

Katherine Katherine Kathrin

Katheun Katheun Katheron

Keturah

Kinboro Kinborough
Kinborrow

Laurentius Lawrence Laurint
Lazarus ‖Laurentus Lanedro
Leonardg Lenard Lenard
Leonard Leondus Lenard ⌈Letitia ✳
Lotitia Littere Lettippa Lettis
Lettis Lotter Lottins Lottere Lottis
Hewies Lowes Lowes Longleroft
Lidia Lodin Lidra Lydia Ludia
Liddia Lodia Lidda
Lucas Lucas ⌈Lucea Luria
Hure Lurye Luce Luce Luro Hure
Lodowirg Lodowius
Curiß Cnriß ✳ Latiβ

48

Mandlen mandlen Mandolinus mugdalen

Mawde mando mando mawde

Malilda

Mawricius Morriro morires Moris

Morris Morrirs Mawris

Molison

Mollior mollian Molior Melior

Mossar Moshar

Mirhell

Miriam

Morgan Morganus

mvses moyses Moses Muses moyses

margaret   Margreat   Margreatt

margaritt   Marygrate   Margerritl

Marffrett   Maeffrett   Marffot   margrete

Margred   Mgareta   Marga^{t}   marieure

margery   Margorie   Margeri

markte mariorus ¶ Margere   Margery

Marhen   Martine   martin

Martha   martha   Martha

Mary   Marysa   maz   Marion

Marion   Maro   Marri   Marri

Mathewe   Mathewe   Mathew

Matheu   Matzow   Mathew   matow

Mathyas   ¶ Mathew

Nathan

Nathanioll Nathanuell Nathaniell

Nicholas Nicholaus Nicholas
Nicolaus Nirklis Nichus nick:
Nicholaus Michalas Nichus
Nichus Nickas

Oliverus Oliu Oliver

Osmundz Osmandus

Oswoll Oswoll Oswoll
Oswoll Oswald
Ewen Owinus Owyn
owen Ozer

Payence Pationtia Patrick

Paule Paule paulus Pole

Paull

Pennollope Penelope Penelopie

Penolopy Penelope

Petrus potter Petter Petter

Phillop Phillus philippe Phio

Phillip Philippus Gilippus

Phus Philla Phus Philla

Phebe Phebe Phebe Phebe

Pristilla Chrystyla Prossilla

Prisilla Prissilla Prosilla Prossilla

Prudonce prudom prudens

Raphaell Raphell Rarhill Raphell

Radulphus Radphus Raphus Rafe

Ralph Ralphe Ralphe Ralfe

Raphael

Rebearka Rebarka Reberka Reberah

Rebara Rebarah Rebera Reberah

Rebekkah Rebebah

Richard Richerd Richdard Rychard

Richard Ricus Ricus Ricus Rici Ric

Richus Rachard Richard

Robart Robert Roblo Robti Robtus

Roberta Robtus Robart Robati Robart

Rohoart Robt

Roger Roger R^coger

Rosmond Rosimond

Ruth

Rowland

Samson Sampsonnd

Shmull Samuel Sammoll

Samuel Sermoll

Saprontia Sapientia

Sussana Sussan Susan Susan

Sitzan Susan Susana Susan

Susanu Suste Sussana susa

Sushana Susann Sussan

Susai Clare Sarrey Sarrey

Sara Sarrah Sarrah

Shadwarh Shadrah

Symon Simon Symon Symon

Simon Simond Symond Symon

Sibboll Sible Sibilla Sibilla

Silfoster

Sallomon ſolomu Sulomon

Elſtephus enſhephanus Steuen

Stoonen Steuen Stephus

Stouon Stephen ſteven

Swithianm Swithen

Tabitha

Theodorus

Theofilus Theophilus Theophil

Theophilus Theophilus Theophilus

Theophillous Theophilus

Thomas Thomas Thomas Thomas Tho:
Thom Thomas Thomas Thomas
Thomas Tomse Thomas Thom

Tamson Tamson Tomeson Tamsyne
sonizon Tomzo Tomsyn Tomezin
Thamisina Tomzon Tomsyne

58

Timothy Tymothy Tymothy

Tomolzy Tym Timotheus

Tobid Tobias Hoboy Tobia'

Toby Toby Tobye

Tristram Trestram Cristrumus

Tristram

Valentine Valentine
Valentinus Valentin
vincent Vmcent
Vortue Vorttue vortue
Uriah   Vortue

Vrith a Vrie ury

Vrsula verdtter Vrolla
Vrsule Vsly Vrssilla
Vrsilla Vrsilla Vrsilly Vrsly
Vrsilla Vrcilla Vrsilly

Walterus Walter Wallew

Waltur walter Gualterus

Wonesside

William Willmus Willms Wm

Willm willms willia Willi

Wilyam will Elliit William Wm

William Willolmus Willm

Guliolmus Guliolmus

Willms Willmm

Χρ̃ian Χρian Χρiana

Χρ̃ar X'ρian Χρibua

Χρ̃ofor Χροfrus Χροfori

Χρouor Χρ̃ofans Χρofher

yedeth

Zacham Zacharias

Zakaria

Abbreviations & words common to Parish Registers

‾ over a letter indicates omission of "M" or "N".

~ over a letter indicates the omission of more than one letter, either before or after, or both before and after, the letter so marked.

9 Initially represents "con", "com", or "cog" :~
9ge = compare ; 9uent = convent ; 9noen=cognomen

9 Finally represents "-us", "-et" :~
Tœrmin9 = Terminus ; ſcilicet = scilicet

9 Attached to the end of any letter but "ꝑ" represents "er", "re", "or" or "ir"; when used finally it represents "us" or "-os" [usually Latin]
Tin9 = Terminus ; Ptū = tortum ; Esqꝛ9 = Esquire

9 Attached to "ꝑ" represents "pre" or "prae" :~
ꝑdc̃us or ꝑdict9 = praedictus ; ꝑsͭ = presbyter

ℇ Finally represents "-es", "-is" or "-s" :~
ꝑntℇ = praesentis ; Custodℇ = custodes

ⁱ A superscript letter often indicates the omission of an "r" ~ cⁱcuit = circuit ; mᵃch = march

ꝝ Finally "-rum" :~ Saꝝ = Sarum.

Some Surnames.

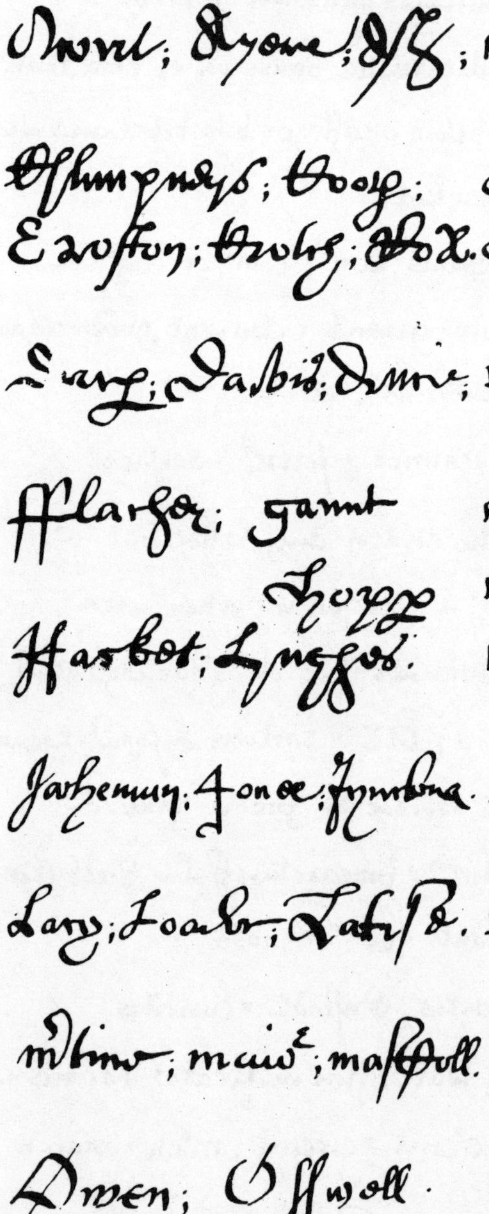

A'COURT; AYERS; ASH.

CHAMPNEYS; COOPER.

CROFTON; CROTCH; COX.

DRAPER; DAVIS; DRUCE.

FLACHER; GAUNT

HOPPER

HACKET; HUGHES

JACKEMAN; JONES; JENKENS

LACY; LOADER; LATISE

MARTINE; MAJOR; MASCOLL

OWEN; OSWELL

PRIOR; PRIOR; PARSONS.

PICK

QUEELL.

ROGERS; ROMESYE

SHEPPERD;

TRACY; TURNER; TURNER

VOULES

WILLIAMS

A 𝕻 𝕻 𝕻 [a] 𝕳 𝕳 𝕳 𝕳 [H] 𝒸𝒻 [cf]

a 𝓊 𝓊 𝓊 [u] [n] 𝓆 [q] 𝒶 [ci] 𝒶 𝒶 [et] 𝑜 [o]

B 𝓛 𝓛 [L] 𝒽 [h]

b 𝓑 𝓑 [v] 𝒽 [h] 𝓑 [ck]

C 𝑂 [o] 𝓓 𝓓 [D] 𝓵 [l] 𝓔 [c] 𝓒 [g] 𝓔 [e] 𝒳 [x]

c 𝓯 [t] 𝓈 𝓈 [s] 𝓇 𝓇 𝓇 [r] 𝓋 [v]

D 𝓐 𝓑 [A] 𝓛 [L] 𝓥 [V] 𝓢 [s] 𝓞 [o] 𝓧 𝓧 [x]

d 𝒹 𝒹 [cl] 𝒹 [s]

E 𝓬 [c] 𝓮 [c] 𝓕 [F] 𝓒 [o,c] 𝓮 𝓮 [k]

e 𝑜 [o] 𝓬 [c] 𝒶 [a] 𝒹 [d] 𝓋 [v] 𝓏 [z]

F 𝓐 [A] 𝓗 [H] 𝓗 [H] 𝓕 [T] 𝒻 [I] 𝒻𝒻 [ss]

f 𝒻 [s]

G 𝓑 𝓑 [B] 𝓑 [b] 𝓒 [c] 𝑜 [o] 𝓮 [e]

g 𝓎 𝓎 𝓎 [y] 𝓆 𝓰 𝓰 [q] 𝓏 [z]

H 𝓛𝓎 𝓱𝓎 [Ly] 𝓖 [G] 𝓑 [B] 𝓗 [ss] 𝓐 [A] 𝒻 [s]

h 𝓮 [e] 𝒻 [f,s,l] 𝓖 [G] 𝓒 [c]

I J 𝓕 𝓕 [F] 𝓨 [T] 𝒻 𝒻 [s] 𝓰 [g] 𝓗 [st,ss]

i 𝓋 𝓋 [v] minims

k 𝓛 [L] 𝓡 𝓡 [R] 𝓑 [B] 𝓑· [B]

k 𝓑 [B] 𝓵 [ll] 𝓵 [t] 𝓱 𝓱 [h]

66

L ℓ ℘ ℘ [p] e [e] ℎ [h]

l ſ [ſ] C ſ [c] ℓℓ [ll] c [c] ℬ [ß] l [t]

M ℳ [w] ℳ [N]

m uu [in, ni] minims

N ſ₂ ſ₂ [p] ℍ [H] ſ [st, sc] ℛℛ [R] ℴc [v]

n u u [u] η ɣ [y] minims

O ꝺꝺ [D] ℭ [c] ℴℓ [e] ℰℬ [G]

o θ [e] o [a] ƺ [s] v [v]

P ɲ [H] ℘ [v] ƴs [js] ℘ [x] ℘ℓ [hs]

þ ƹ ℱ [x] þ [twm þ]

Q ℂ ℂ [G]

q ɣ ℊ ℊ ℸ [g] ℊ ℊ [abrev "conḡ "us"] ꝙ

R ℞ [ß] ℱ [F] ℛ [w] ℱ [k] ℙ [n]

r ⅍ℓ [e] ʒʒʒ [z] z [z] x [x] v [v]

S θ [o] ℚ [A] ℚ [Q] ℓ [c] ℭ [G]

s ſ ſ [ſ] ʄ [j] ℓ [st]

T ℙ [p] ℰ [E] ℺ [o, c] ℓℓℓ [s] ℛ [A]

t ℓ [c] ℓ ℓ [e] ℓ ℓ ℓ [t]

UV minims ℒ [L] ℒℓ [w]

v ℬ ℓ [b] ℘ [x]

W [LB] [EB] [EB] [LX]

w [n] minims

X [Y] [P]

x [P]

Y [X] [P thorn]

y [8] [z] [abbrev "Rum"]

Z see "r"

z [abbrev. "que".]

NUMBERS & DATES

1	Januarij
2	ffebruarij
3	Marcij
4	Aprillis or Apris
5	Maij
6	Junij
7	Julij
8	Augusti
9	Septembris
10	Octobris
11	Novembris
1661 = ; 1678 =	Decembris
1691 = or	

Alias = *(abbreviations)* als ; aliud ; als ; alts ; alts ; alios ; Elis

And = *(abbreviation symbols)*

Anno Domini = Anno Dm̄ ; Aº Dm̄ ; anº dom̄ ;

Anno Regni Regis : *(abbreviations)* ; rr
    Anno R R ; Anno Regni Reg⁷ Anno regni Regis

Baptized = bapt ; batiz ; baptiz ; baptiz ; Baptiz
    baptizedq ; baptizatus ; Baptizabantur
    baptizator ; baptizata

Church wardens : Church Wardens ; Custo Ecclie
    Custodie Ecclie ; Custodes Ecclie.

Curate : *(abbreviation)*

December : Xber ; xbr ; jober

Et : *(abbreviation symbols)*

Et cetera : *(abbreviation symbols)*

Esquire : *(abbreviations)* ; E Squir⁵ ; E Squir ;

Eodem die ; same day = Eodem die ; eode Die

69

fil: fillia; filius; fi9 - son or daughter (Filius Terrae
[Filius Terrae = bastard]

Generosus (a) = gen; gent; Gendros

humatus; humatus; inhumatus (a) = BURIED

Infant = Infans;
Junior = jun^E;

Married = matr^E & copulabat^E; Matri: cupulat;
mat. lit. copulati; in matrimonium copul-
abantur; maried; married; Nuptiae

Minister = mynister; mnnsts;

November = 9ber;
Nuper; Nup? = nuper ~ the late; lately

October = 8ber

℈ represents "per", "par" or "por":—
℈mit = permit; ℈ties = parties; ℈ch = porch
℈ represents "pro":— ℈bat, ℈b = probate.
℈ r̃ = proximus; ℈fessor = professor.

70

parish · *manuscript forms* : Parish

parsons= *manuscript forms*

presents = *manuscript forms*

provided = *manuscript forms*

Sancti = *manuscript forms*

Senior = *manuscript forms*

Sepulta (-us) ; Sepoliobat *manuscript forms* · buried

Several = *manuscript forms* .
September = *manuscript forms*
Spurius ~ bastard : *manuscript forms*

vicar : *manuscript forms* ;
Widow = *manuscript forms*